3

Look and See

Susannah Reed

NATIONAL GEOGRAPHIC
LEARNING

Australia • Brazil • Mexico • Singapore • United Kingdom • United States

Scope and Sequence

		Words	Structure	Value	Phonics	Content Connections	
						Video	Project
1 **In Class** p. 5		count to ten draw a picture make a craft play a game read a book sing a song write letters	Let's draw a picture. OK, good idea!/ No, thanks.	Work hard at school.	cat, rat	**Math** How does addition work?	An abacus
2 **Weather** p. 11		rainy cloudy cold hot snowy sunny windy	What's the weather like? It's sunny.	Be careful in the sun.	man, van	**Science** Where does rain come from?	A water cycle diagram
3 **My Community** p. 17		firefighter bus driver dentist doctor librarian mail carrier police officer vet	Is he/she a doctor? Yes, he/she is./ No, he/she isn't.	Be polite.	bed, red	**Social Science** How do people in the community help us?	A community helper book
4 **Make Some Noise!** p. 23		drums guitar piano recorder tambourine trumpet violin xylophone	He can play the piano. She can play the guitar.	Work together.	pet, vet	**Music** What types of musical instruments are there?	A drum
5 **Shapes Around Us** p. 29		circle diamond hexagon oval rectangle square star triangle	What are these? They're diamonds.	Use your imagination.	mix, six	**Math** What are the 3D shapes around us?	A pyramid

Back to School

Monday

Tuesday

Wednesday

Thursday

Friday

Saturday

Sunday

What day is it today?

It's Monday.

REVIEW: *Back to School*   **STRUCTURE**: *What day is it today? It's Monday.*

1 TR: 0.1 Listen and point. Say.   **2** TR: 0.2 Listen and chant.   **3** TR: 0.3 Listen and say.

In Class

Students learning numbers, Vietnam

LESSON 1

NEW WORDS: *count to ten*

1 Look and see.   **2** SC: 1 Watch.   **3** TR: 1.1 Listen and say.   **4** TR: 1.2 Listen and do.

5

read a book

make a craft

play a game

draw a picture

write letters

sing a song

I can read a book.

LESSON 2

NEW WORDS: *draw a picture, make a craft, play a game, read a book, sing a song, write letters*

1 TR: 1.3 Listen and point. **2** TR: 1.4 Listen and say. **3** TR: 1.5 Listen and chant. **4** Point and say.

LESSON 3

STRUCTURE: *Let's draw a picture. OK, good idea!/No, thanks.*

1 TR: 1.6 **Listen and circle.**   **2** TR: 1.7 **Listen and say.**   **3** Play and say.

7

SONG AND VALUE: *Work hard at school.*

1 TR: 1.8 Listen and point.   **2** TR: 1.9 Listen and sing.   **3** TR: 1.10 Sing and do.   **4** Stick.

LESSON 4

VALUE

Work hard at school.

cat

rat

PHONICS: *cat* and *rat*

1 TR: 1.11 Listen and point. **2** TR: 1.12 Listen and say. **3** TR: 1.13 Listen and chant. **4** Stick and say. Match.

9

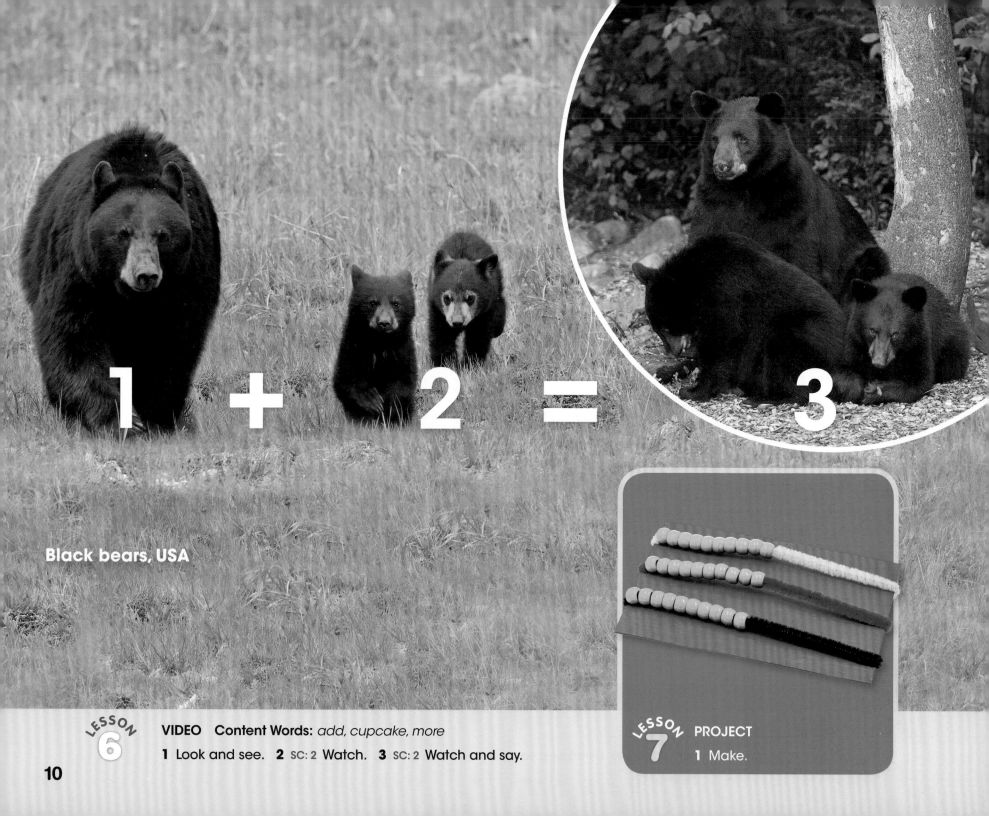

1 + 2 = 3

Black bears, USA

LESSON 6

VIDEO   Content Words: *add, cupcake, more*

1 Look and see.   **2** SC: 2 Watch.   **3** SC: 2 Watch and say.

LESSON 7   PROJECT

1 Make.

Weather

An orangutan on a
rainy day, Indonesia

LESSON 1

NEW WORD: *rainy*

1 Look and see.   **2** SC: 3 Watch.   **3** TR: 2.1 Listen and say.   **4** TR: 2.2 Listen and do.

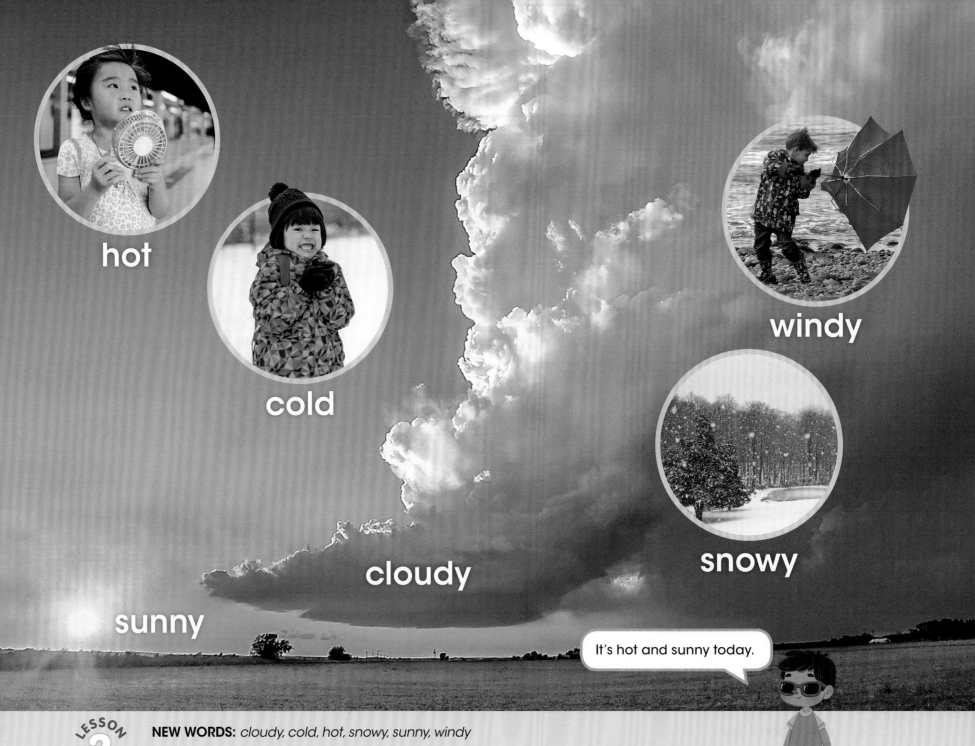

hot

cold

windy

snowy

cloudy

sunny

It's hot and sunny today.

LESSON 2

NEW WORDS: *cloudy, cold, hot, snowy, sunny, windy*

1 TR: 2.3 Listen and point. **2** TR: 2.4 Listen and say. **3** TR: 2.5 Listen and chant. **4** Look and say.

END

START

What's the weather like?

It's sunny.

LESSON 3

STRUCTURE: *What's the weather like? It's sunny.*

1 TR: 2.6 Listen and point. **2** TR: 2.7 Listen and say. **3** Play and say.

13

Boys hiking in the Alps, Switzerland

LESSON 4

SONG AND VALUE: *Be careful in the sun.*

1 TR: 2.8 Listen and point.   **2** TR: 2.9 Listen and sing.   **3** TR: 2.10 Sing and do.   **4** Stick.

VALUE

Be careful in the sun.

m a n

man

v a n

van

m a n ○ ○

v a n ○ ○

LESSON 5

PHONICS: *man* and *van*

1 TR: 2.11 Listen and point. **2** TR: 2.12 Listen and say. **3** TR: 2.13 Listen and chant. **4** Stick and say. Match.

15

Clouds and heavy rain,
Austria

LESSON 6

VIDEO Content Words: *cloud, down, rain, steam, up*

1 Look and see.   **2** SC:4 Watch.   **3** SC:4 Watch, point, and say.

LESSON 7

PROJECT

1 Make.

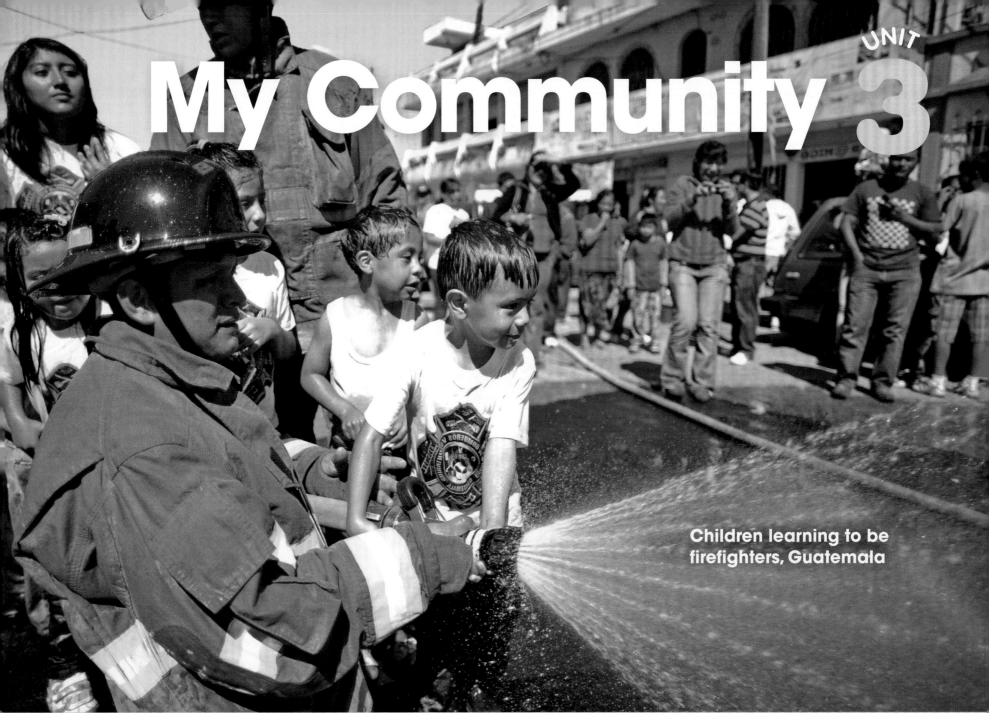

My Community

Children learning to be firefighters, Guatemala

LESSON 1

NEW WORD: *firefighter*

1 Look and see. **2** SC: 5 Watch. **3** TR: 3.1 Listen and say. **4** TR: 3.2 Listen and do.

17

mail carrier

librarian

police officer

bus driver

dentist

doctor

vet

He's a doctor.

NEW WORDS: *bus driver, dentist, doctor, librarian, mail carrier, police officer, vet*

1 TR: 3.3 Listen and point. **2** TR: 3.4 Listen and say. **3** TR: 3.5 Listen and chant. **4** Point and say.

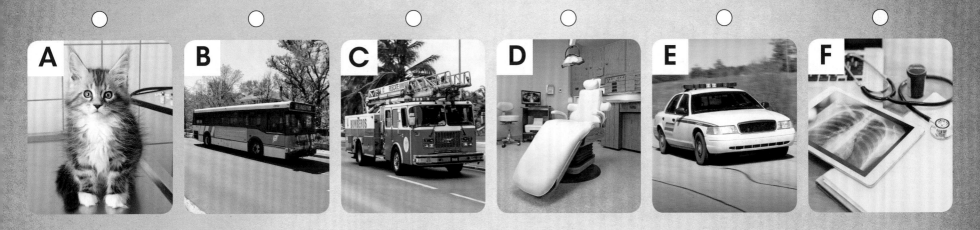

STRUCTURE: *Is he/she a doctor? Yes, he/she is./No, he/she isn't.*

1 TR: 3.6 **Listen and match.**   **2** TR: 3.7 **Listen and say.**   **3 Play and say.**

19

A friendly bus driver, USA

VALUE

Be polite.

LESSON 4

SONG AND VALUE: *Be polite.*

1 TR: 3.8 Listen and point.　**2** TR: 3.9 Listen and sing.　**3** TR: 3.10 Sing and do.　**4** Stick.

b e d **r e d**

red

bed

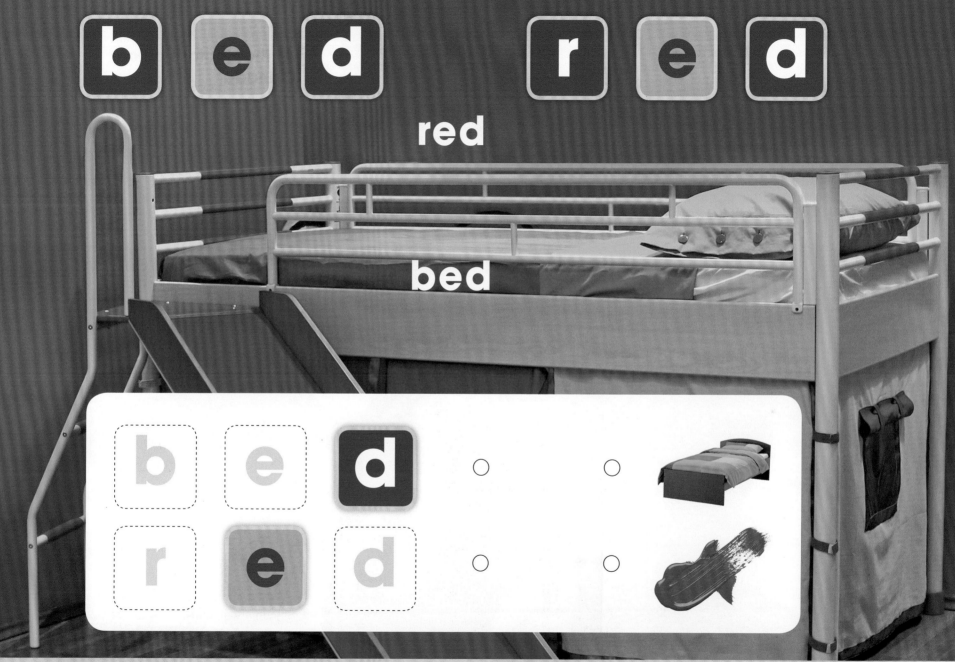

PHONICS: *bed* and *red*

1 TR: 3.11 Listen and point. **2** TR: 3.12 Listen and say. **3** TR: 3.13 Listen and chant. **4** Stick and say. Match.

At the doctor's office,
Canada

MY COMMUNITY

LESSON
6

VIDEO   Content Words: *help, people*

1 Look and see.   **2** SC: 6 Watch.   **3** SC: 6 Watch and say.

LESSON
7

PROJECT

1 Make.

Make Some Noise!

Women playing drums, South Korea

NEW WORD: *drums*

1 Look and see. **2** SC: 7 Watch. **3** TR: 4.1 Listen and say. **4** TR: 4.2 Listen and do.

Mariachi musicians, Mexico

trumpet

guitar

violin

tambourine

recorder

xylophone

piano

I can play the tambourine.

LESSON 2

NEW WORDS: *guitar, piano, recorder, tambourine, trumpet, violin, xylophone*

1 TR: 4.3 Listen and point. **2** TR: 4.4 Listen and say. **3** TR: 4.5 Listen and chant. **4** Point and say.

24

STRUCTURE: *He can play the piano. She can play the guitar.*

1 TR: 4.6 Listen and follow. **2** TR: 4.7 Listen and say. **3** Play and say.

LESSON
3

25

A music class, Canada

VALUE

Work together.

LESSON 4

SONG AND VALUE: *Work together.*

1 TR: 4.8 Listen and point.   2 TR: 4.9 Listen and sing.   3 TR: 4.10 Sing and do.   4 Stick.

p e t

v e t

vet

pet

p e t

v e t

PHONICS: *pet* and *vet*

1 TR: 4.11 Listen and point.　**2** TR: 4.12 Listen and say.　**3** TR: 4.13 Listen and chant.　**4** Stick and say. Match.

LESSON 6

VIDEO Content Words: *percussion, stringed, wind*

1 Look and see. **2** SC: 8 Watch. **3** SC: 8 Watch, point, and say.

7 **PROJECT**

1 Make.

Shapes Around Us

Girl walking on circles, Portugal

LESSON 1

NEW WORD: *circle*

1 Look and see.　**2** SC: 9 Watch.　**3** TR: 5.1 Listen and say.　**4** TR: 5.2 Listen and do.

oval

hexagon

square

triangle

star

diamond

rectangle

I can draw a star.

NEW WORDS: *diamond, hexagon, oval, rectangle, square, star, triangle*

1 TR: 5.3 Listen and point. **2** TR: 5.4 Listen and say. **3** TR: 5.5 Listen and chant. **4** Draw and say.

What are these?

They're diamonds.

Origami animals

Use your
imagination.

SONG AND VALUE: *Use your imagination.*

1 TR: 5.8 Listen and point.   **2** TR: 5.9 Listen and sing.   **3** TR: 5.10 Sing and do.   **4** Stick.

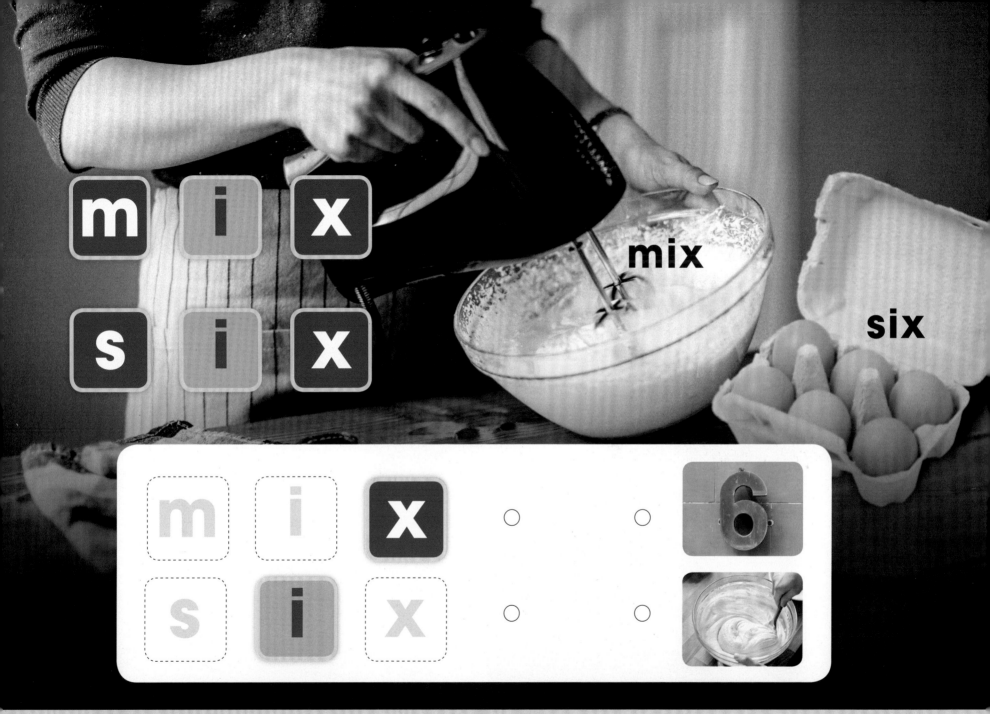

m i x

s i x

mix

six

m i **x**

s **i** x

6

PHONICS: *mix* and *six*

1 TR: 5.11 Listen and point. **2** TR: 5.12 Listen and say. **3** TR: 5.13 Listen and chant. **4** Stick and say. Match.

VIDEO Content Words: *cube, flat, pyramid, sphere, world*

1 Look and see. **2** SC: 10 Watch. **3** SC: 10 Watch, point, and say.

PROJECT

1 Make.

Can You Swim?

A baby learning to swim, USA

LESSON 1

NEW WORD: *swim*

1 Look and see. **2** SC: 11 Watch. **3** TR: 6.1 Listen and say. **4** TR: 6.2 Listen and do.

35

skip

ride

Two colorful macaws, Bolivia

fly

kick

climb

throw

catch

I can catch a ball.

LESSON 2

NEW WORDS: *catch, climb, fly, kick, ride, skip, throw*

1 TR: 6.3 Listen and point.   **2** TR: 6.4 Listen and say.   **3** TR: 6.5 Listen and chant.   **4** Point and say.

1   **2**   **3**

Can you skip?

Can you ride a scooter?

Yes, I can.

No, I can't.

LESSON 3

STRUCTURE: *Can you skip? Yes, I can./No, I can't.*
1 TR: 6.6 Listen and point.   **2** TR: 6.7 Listen and say.   **3** Play and say.

37

Children climbing a tree, Norway

VALUE

Try again.

LESSON 4

SONG AND VALUE: *Try again.*

1 TR: 6.8 Listen and point.   **2** TR: 6.9 Listen and sing.   **3** TR: 6.10 Sing and do.   **4** Stick.

b i g   d i g

big   dig

b i **g**

d **i** g

LESSON 5

PHONICS: *big* and *dig*

1 TR: 6.11 Listen and point. **2** TR: 6.12 Listen and say. **3** TR: 6.13 Listen and chant. **4** Stick and say. Match.

LESSON 6

VIDEO Content Word: *penguin*

1 Look and see. **2** SC: 12 Watch. **3** SC: 12 Watch, point, and say.

LESSON 7

PROJECT

1 Make.

At Home

Homes in a small village, Greenland

LESSON 1

NEW WORD: *welcome*

1 Look and see.   **2** SC: 13 Watch.   **3** TR: 7.1 Listen and say.   **4** TR: 7.2 Listen and do.

shelf

bed

sink

kitchen

bedroom

bathroom

living room

sofa

Where's the sofa?

It's in the living room.

NEW WORDS: *bathroom, bedroom, kitchen, living room; bed, shelf, sink, sofa*

1 TR: 7.3 Listen and point.   **2** TR: 7.4 Listen and say.   **3** TR: 7.5 Listen and chant.   **4** Point and say.

1

2

The picture is under the bed.

The picture is in the bathroom.

The cars are on the chair.

The cars are under the bed.

LESSON 3

STRUCTURE: *The picture is in the bathroom. The cars are under the bed.*

1 TR: 7.6 Listen and point. **2** TR: 7.7 Listen and say. **3** Play and say.

43

Boy helping at home,
Sweden

VALUE

Help at home.

SONG AND VALUE: *Help at home.*

1 TR: 7.8 Listen and point. **2** TR: 7.9 Listen and sing. **3** TR: 7.10 Sing and do. **4** Stick.

d o g

l o g

dog

log

d o **g** ○ ○

l **o** g ○ ○

PHONICS: *dog* and *log*

1 TR: 7.11 Listen and point. **2** TR: 7.12 Listen and say. **3** TR: 7.13 Listen and chant. **4** Stick and say. Match.

 VIDEO **Content Words:** *apartment, city, country, garden, house*

1 Look and see. **2** SC: 14 Watch. **3** SC: 14 Watch and say.

LESSON **7** **PROJECT**

1 Make.

46

My Special Place

8

A group of tree houses

NEW WORD: *tree house*

1 Look and see. **2** SC: 15 Watch. **3** TR: 8.1 Listen and say. **4** TR: 8.2 Listen and do.

lamp

toy box

window

door

pillow

blanket

rug

I have a blanket in my special place.

LESSON 2

NEW WORDS: *blanket, door, lamp, pillow, rug, toy box, window*

1 TR: 8.3 Listen and point.　**2** TR: 8.4 Listen and say.　**3** TR: 8.5 Listen and chant.　**4** Point and say.

Is there a rug?

Yes, there is.

Is there a teddy bear?

No, there isn't.

LESSON 3

STRUCTURE: *Is there a rug? Yes, there is./No, there isn't.*

1 TR: 8.6 Listen and point.   **2** TR: 8.7 Listen and say.   **3** Play and say.

49

Boys in a tent, USA

VALUE

Be welcoming.

SONG AND VALUE: *Be welcoming.*

1 TR: 8.8 **Listen and point.** **2** TR: 8.9 **Listen and sing.** **3** TR: 8.10 **Sing and do.** **4** Stick.

box

fox

PHONICS: *box* and *fox*

LESSON 5

1 TR: 8.11 Listen and point.   **2** TR: 8.12 Listen and say.   **3** TR: 8.13 Listen and chant.   **4** Stick and say. Match.

LESSON 6

VIDEO   **Content Words:** *hole, nest, squirrel*

1 Look and see.   **2** SC: 16 Watch.   **3** SC: 16 Watch, point, and say.

7 PROJECT

1 Make.

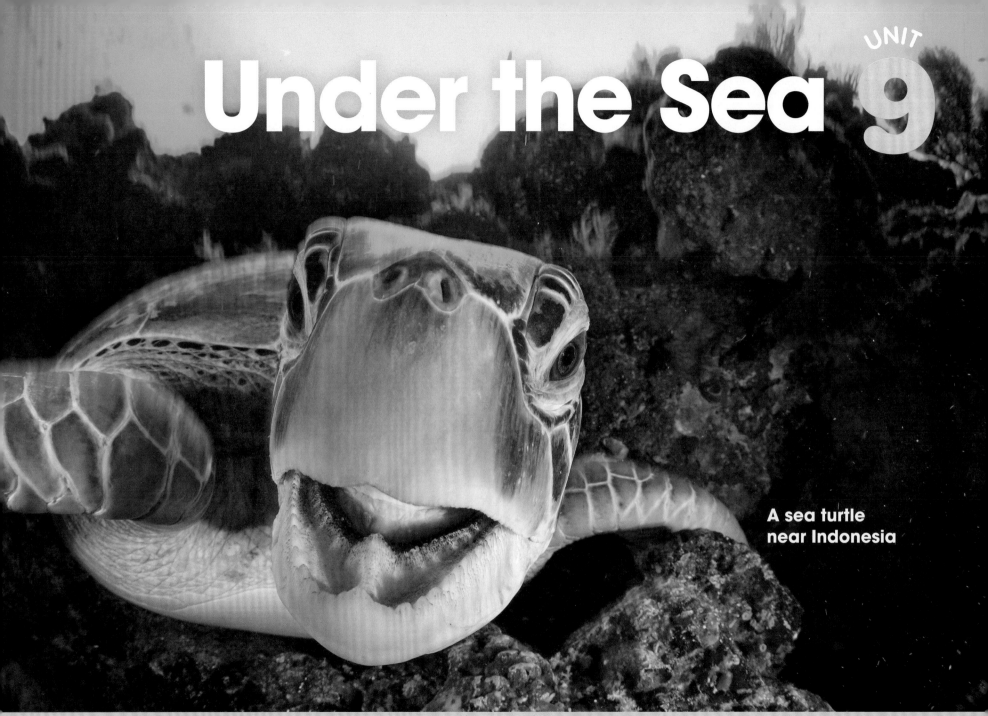

Under the Sea

A sea turtle
near Indonesia

LESSON 1

NEW WORD: *turtle*

1 Look and see. **2** SC: 17 Watch. **3** TR: 9.1 Listen and say. **4** TR: 9.2 Listen and do.

53

crab

seahorse

octopus

shark

starfish

jellyfish

dolphin

There's a yellow seahorse.

LESSON 2

NEW WORDS: *crab, dolphin, jellyfish, octopus, seahorse, shark, starfish*

1 TR: 9.3 Listen and point. **2** TR: 9.4 Listen and say. **3** TR: 9.5 Listen and chant. **4** Point and say.

54

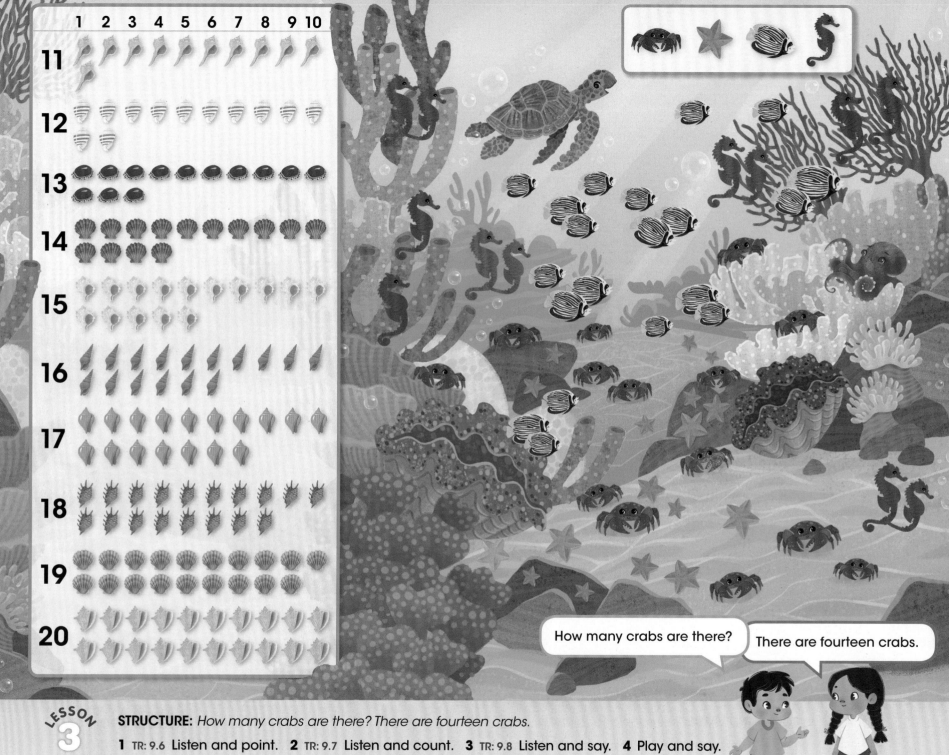

LESSON 3

STRUCTURE: *How many crabs are there? There are fourteen crabs.*

1 TR: 9.6 Listen and point. **2** TR: 9.7 Listen and count. **3** TR: 9.8 Listen and say. **4** Play and say.

55

SONG AND VALUE: *Keep the beach clean.*

1 TR: 9.9 Listen and point.   **2** TR: 9.10 Listen and sing.   **3** TR: 9.11 Sing and do.   **4** Stick.

VALUE

Keep the beach clean.

sun

run

r u n

s u n

LESSON 5

PHONICS: *run* and *sun*

1 TR: 9.12 Listen and point.   **2** TR: 9.13 Listen and say.   **3** TR: 9.14 Listen and chant.   **4** Stick and say. Match.

57

A shark in a coral reef near the Bahamas

LESSON 6 VIDEO Content Words: *beautiful, coral reef, eat*
1 Look and see. 2 SC: 18 Watch. 3 SC: 18 Watch and say.

LESSON 7 PROJECT
1 Make.

Picnic Time

A picnic near the beach, Oman

LESSON 1

NEW WORD: *picnic*

1 Look and see. **2** SC: 19 Watch. **3** TR: 10.1 Listen and say. **4** TR: 10.2 Listen and do.

vegetables

yogurt

lemonade

juice

fruit

cheese

sandwich

I like lemonade.

NEW WORDS: *cheese, fruit, juice, lemonade, sandwich, vegetables, yogurt*

1 TR: 10.3 Listen and point. **2** TR: 10.4 Listen and say. **3** TR: 10.5 Listen and chant. **4** Point and say.

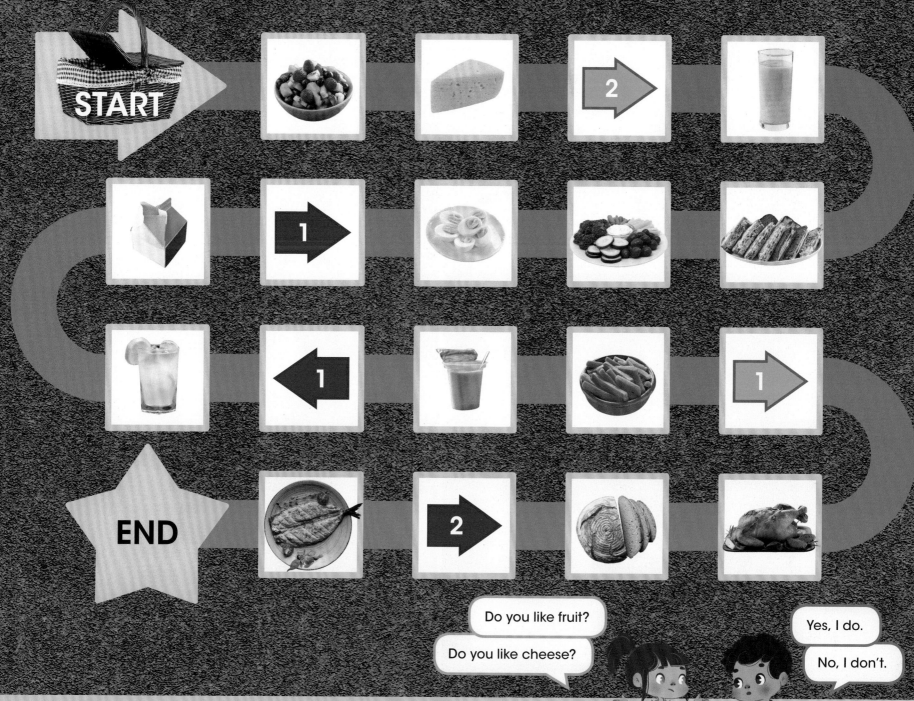

LESSON 3

STRUCTURE: *Do you like fruit? Yes, I do./No, I don't.*

1 TR: 10.6 Listen and point. **2** TR: 10.7 Listen and say. **3** Play and say.

61

LESSON 4

SONG AND VALUE: *Try new things.*

1 TR: 10.8 Listen and point.   **2** TR: 10.9 Listen and sing.   **3** TR: 10.10 Sing and do.   **4** Stick.

62

VALUE

Try new things.

bug

mug

LESSON 5

PHONICS: *bug* and *mug*

1 TR: 10.11 **Listen and point.**   2 TR: 10.12 **Listen and say.**   3 TR: 10.13 **Listen and chant.**   4 **Stick and say. Match.**

63

LESSON 6

VIDEO   Content Words: *dairy, grain, healthy, protein*

1 Look and see.   **2** SC: 20 Watch.   **3** SC: 20 Watch, point, and say.

LESSON 7

PROJECT

1 Make.

In Class

Let's play a game,
play a game.
Let's play a game together.

[Chorus]
Let's work hard.
Let's work hard.
Let's work hard at school.

Let's write letters,
write letters.
Let's write letters together.

[Chorus]

Let's read a book,
read a book.
Let's read a book together.

[Chorus]

Weather

What's the weather like?
It's hot and sunny today.
Here you are, take this sun hat.
It's hot and sunny today.

[Chorus]
Be careful in the sun, today.
Be careful in the sun.

What's the weather like?
It's hot and sunny today.
Here you are, take this water.
It's hot and sunny today.

[Chorus]

What's the weather like?
It's hot and sunny today.
Here you are, take this
sunscreen.
It's hot and sunny today.

[Chorus]

65

Make Some Noise!

I can play the tambourine.
She can play the tambourine.
Let's play the tambourine
together.

[Chorus]
I can play music.
She can play music.
He can play music.
Let's work together.

I can play the drums.
She can play the drums.
Let's play the drums
together.

[Chorus]

I can play the recorder.
She can play the recorder.
Let's play the recorder
together.

[Chorus]

UNIT
3

My Community

This is Mrs. Johnson.
She's a bus driver.
Hello, Mrs. Johnson.
How are you?
How are you today?
I'm fine, thank you.
How are you?
I'm fine, too, thank you!

This is Mr. Olson.
He's a firefighter.
Hello, Mr. Olson.
How are you?
How are you today?
I'm fine, thank you.
How are you?
I'm fine, too, thank you!

This is Dr. Burton.
She's a vet.
Hello, Dr. Burton.
How are you?
How are you today?
I'm fine, thank you.
How are you?
I'm fine, too, thank you!

UNIT
5

Shapes Around Us

What's this?
It's a sheep, a paper sheep.
A paper sheep with shapes.
There are squares and triangles.
There are diamonds, too.

[Chorus]
What are these? They're animals.
They're animals with shapes.
Use your imagination
and make animals with shapes.

What's this?
It's a dinosaur, a paper dinosaur.
A paper dinosaur with shapes.
There's a rectangle and
a hexagon.
There are triangles, too.

[Chorus]

UNIT
6

Can You Swim?

Can you climb a tree?
No, I can't. No, I can't.
I can't climb a tree.
Come on! Yes, you can.
Try and try again.

Look at me! Can you see?
Now I can climb a tree!
Now he can climb a tree!

Can you ride a bike?
No, I can't. No, I can't.
I can't ride a bike.
Come on! Yes, you can.
Try and try again.

Look at me! Can you see?
Now I can ride a bike!
Now she can ride a bike!

8

My Special Place

Welcome to my
special place.
It's my special place.
Is there a window?
No, there isn't.
Is there a door?
No, there isn't.
There's a blanket and
there's a lamp.
It's my special place.

[Chorus]
Here it is, my special place.
Welcome! Come on in.
Come and play with me!

Welcome to my
special place.
It's my special place.
Is there a bed?
No, there isn't.
Is there a toy box?
No, there isn't.
There's a game and
there are trees.
It's my special place.

[Chorus]

UNIT

7

At Home

Look at me. I'm at home.
I'm in my bedroom.
There's a table and
there are toys.
The toys are on the floor.
Let's clean up the bedroom.
Put the toys on the table.
Let's clean up the bedroom.
Let's help at home.

Look at me. I'm at home.
I'm in the kitchen.
There's a sink and
there are dishes.
The dishes are in the sink.
Let's clean up the kitchen.
Put the dishes on the shelf.
Let's clean up the kitchen.
Let's help at home.

68

UNIT
9

Under the Sea

What are these?
They're turtles,
baby turtles on the beach.
How many turtles are there?
There are seven in all.
Let's help the turtles.
Let's keep the beach clean.

What are these?
They're starfish,
colorful starfish on the beach.
How many starfish are there?
There are two in all.
Let's help the starfish.
Let's keep the beach clean.

What's this?
It's a crab,
a small crab on the beach.
How many crabs are there?
There's one, that's all!

Let's help the crab.
Let's keep the beach clean.

UNIT
10

Picnic Time

Do you like cheese?
No, I don't.
Do you like vegetables?
No, I don't.
Do you like sandwiches?
Yes, I do.
You do? That's good!
Here you are.
Here's a sandwich for you.

I like this sandwich!
You do? That's good!
It's a cheese and
vegetable sandwich.
It's good to try new things.

Do you like carrots?
No, I don't.
Do you like oranges?
No, I don't.
Do you like juice?
Yes, I do.
You do? That's good!
Here you are.
Here's some juice for you.

I like this juice!
You do? That's good!
It's carrot and orange juice.
It's good to try new things.

Aa
alligator

Bb
beaver

Cc
camel

Dd
duck

Ii
iguana

Jj
jaguar

Kk
kangaroo

Ll
lion

Qq
quail

Rr
reindeer

Ss
seal

Tt
tiger

Uu
umbrellabird

Ee
elephant

Ff
fish

Gg
gorilla

Hh
hippo

Mm
monkey

Nn
numbat

Oo
octopus

Pp
panda

Vv
vulture

Ww
wolf

Xx
fox

Yy
yak

Zz
zebra

CREDITS

c	a	r	t	m	a	v	n	b	e
r	d	p	e	v	t	m	i	s	x
b	i	d	g	d	o	l	g	b	o
f	x	r	u	s	n	b	u	m	g